DEAR YOU

POEMS THROUGH THE HEART

FROM THE RED PENGUIN COLLECTION

Dear You–Poems Through The Heart

Copyright © 20223 by JK Larkin

All rights reserved

Published by Red Penguin Books

Bellerose Village, New York

Library of Congress Control Number: 2023903981

ISBN

Print 978-1-63777-387-1

Digital 978-1-63777-386-4

No part of this book may be reproduced in any form or by any electronic or mechanical means, including information storage and retrieval systems, without written permission from the author, except for the use of brief quotations in a book review.

CONTENTS

VALENTINE'S DAY HAIKU Shai Afsai	1
ALL I WANTED WAS SOME FUCKING FRUIT Matt Martinek	3
MELISSA'S POEM Shai Afsai	5
OUTRAGEOUS THINGS I WILL NOT DO TODAY – AFTER CHERIE HANSON Sally Quon	7
"NEXT PLACE" Melody Lipford	9
SHIPS Jerri Hardesty	11
FRIEND-ZONED…YET AGAIN David Lange	13
READ RECEIPT Kirstin Kochie	17
THE RENTED ROOM Carella Keil	21
PUSH Michael Artemis	23
NOTHING LEFT Debbie De Louise	25
NOSTALGIA ON A CLOUDY DAY K.V. Raghupathi	27
QUESTIONS Sally Quon	29
BOOKSTORE HAIKU Shai Afsai	31
THE BOY WHO LIVED IN THE FOREST Sally Quon	33
PERMANENT Jerri Hardesty	35

LOVING SHADOWS Henry Vinicio Valerio Madriz	37
EMOTIONAL EXHIBITIONIST Carella Keil	39
PHOTOTROPE Janis Butler Holm	41
...BUT IT IS NOT ALL THAT YOU MAKE AND EXHIBIT K.V. Raghupathi	43
DON'T EVER THINK... Carol Alena Aronoff	47
FOOL'S GOLD Myna Wallin	49
TEDDY BEAR LOVE Michael Artemis	51
TEN YEARS Lisa Diaz Meyer	53
ROAD TRIPS Carella Keil	55
CHOICE Leslie Arambula	57
HEARTBREAKER Jerri Hardesty	59
WITHOUT YOU Candice Louisa Daquin	61
WHEN YOU TOOK AWAY YOUR LOVE Debbie De Louise	63
ERASURE POEM Carella Keil	65
BROKEN Sally Quon	67
HEARTBREAK AISLE Carella Keil	69
EVASION BA Brittingham	71
ANOTHER CHANCE Shai Afsai	73
CALLOUS BA Brittingham	75

DEAR MISTAKES 77
Mary C. M. Phillips

PAST LIVES 79
Dion O'Reilly

AND SO CATHERINE HOWARD PRACTICED LAYING
HER HEAD ON THE BLOCK, TO TRY THE FACE SHE
WOULD PULL WHEN THE AXE FELL, OR PERHAPS TO
SIMULATE A SLEEPLESS NIGHT 81
Michael Artemis

(BUT THEN AGAIN) 83
Linda M. Crate

GHOST IN MY REARVIEW MIRROR 85
Melody Lipford

SENRYU (TO THE CURB) 87
Jerri Hardesty

SORRY, NOT SORRY 89
Sally Quon

I WILL NEVER THANK YOU 91
Linda M. Crate

I SIT INSIDE DUSK 93
Carella Keil

A WOLF WITHOUT PROTECTION 97
Linda M. Crate

THE HOUSE OF ECHOES 99
N.E Salmon

AFTER ALL THIS TIME 101
Michelle Chermaine Ramos

REGRETS 105
Anna Sanderson

NOW I AM GRATEFUL 107
Linda M. Crate

CLOSURE 109
Carol Alena Aronoff

WOKEN, NOT BROKEN 111
Michelle Chermaine Ramos

About the Authors 113
Also from The Red Penguin Collection 123

"The heart was made to be broken."
–*Oscar Wilde*

Valentine's Day Haiku
   – Shai Afsai

alone with a new moon
and glass of wine –
I've felt worse

all I wanted was some fucking fruit
   – Matt Martinek

And there you were, that bright angel face
ascending over the tops of the cantaloupes
I was inspecting so closely.
Startled is not the word.
I would have hidden behind the rotting bananas had I spotted you.
How do you speak after 15 years of nothingness, filled with only fantasy
and the fleeting glimpses of could-have-beens?
What do you say? I'm sorry? We would have been great together?
Do I need to tell you that I think about you all the time and pretend you are my wife
and I am your husband
and we are the sexy couple on the crinkled postcard from Hawaii
that always falls from the fridge into the dog dish
because our magnets are crap?
The worst possible thing happens…you give me a hug and I find out that
you wear that same hypnotic perfume from high school
I wished I would wake up to someday, maybe everyday.
We speak on unimportant things…our childhood school is now a parking lot,
how you're making it work in Philly and I am doing wonderful back at home,
and all the while I am scoping out those tanned legs,
thinking of how well they would wrap around my waist.
You know, I know, but we stop just short of pure truth,
that awkward moment arriving when the words cease
and we speak only through our eyes, our cue
to retreat with the usual nod and well wishes.
You proceed to the checkout line, your front wheel
on the grocery cart screeching horribly and wobbling,
just as they always do.

MATT MARTINEK

Your back being turned to me, I mouth the words
"I love you" in silence.

Melissa's Poem
 – *Shai Afsai*

Mom is scheduled to call
in about an hour.
I open a bottle of wine.

———

On the second date,
I express an opinion.
It's over.

———

I meet up with three friends for cocktails,
just like the girls from *Sex and the City* –
except we're not in New York, and I don't like my friends.

———

Making the bed alone,
the sheets won't stay in place.
But he never helped with that either.

———

Clearly the woman on the mat to my right
is convinced deodorant and yoga
are mutually exclusive.

———

He explains that women keep living longer
and men are dying younger.
I sleep with him anyway.

———

Now I have a thing for guys with beards –
but after a few weeks or a month, I push them to shave.
They do, and we break up soon after.

———

Driving back from my sister's,
I remember:
I hated her even when we were kids.

———

He's muscled, with arms covered in tattoos,

and tells me the more he looks like an ex-con,
the more women are drawn to him. I'm drawn.

———

He tells me he divorced his second wife after she allowed
his stepdaughter to buy a pet rabbit over his objections.
Somehow this makes sense to me.

———

He says he spent three months in the far east,
and that yoga changed his life.
I trick myself into believing I've met someone interesting.

———

He's twelve years older. Before #MeToo, I'd have told women
he was my former high school teacher, just to get a reaction,
and half of them would've said, "That's hot!"

———

Xanax inside
the white pharmacy bag –
no need to die now.

Outrageous Things I Will Not Do Today – after Cherie Hanson
  – Sally Quon

I will not buy the twelve-dollar dress I found on-line,
all flounces and lace –
the one that reminds me of Stevie Nicks
and would look ridiculous on my aging body.
I will not sit cross-legged on my bed
Surrounded by piles of cheap fabric
or dance alone in my living room with shades up
so neighbors can watch me twirl.

I will not sneak off to the beach at midnight
shedding clothes at waters edge.
Dive into the waves, let cool water caress me,
white belly and breasts shimmering
like silver fish in the moonlight.

I will not call my former lover,
Relent,
say, "Yes. You can come,"
even though I dreamed of him last night –
splattered with mud and pink paint.
When he pulled me into his arms
and the tip of his tongue lightly touched mine,

I could taste him once again.

"Next Place"
   – Melody Lipford

Dear You,

There's been a little heartache,
a little bit of bitterness.
A whole lot of hardly,
a nice dose of missing it.
And imperfect timing with some miscommunications.
Such as messages never received.
However, as inconvenient as it has been.

I am not grieved.

Instead, I'm happily,
face-front driving up
to the next place
I'm meant to run.

This chapter, this season is almost done.
I've sung the melody.
And now this song has reached its final note.
And I'm grateful for the lessons I've learned.

But now,
It's on to the next place,
To see who I become.

There's been a little bit of anger.
A little bit of I don't get it.
A whole lot of the unexpected.
But, then how could I not see it?
Coming up around me,
the clues all pointed clearly…
a vision I refused to see.

MELODY LIPFORD

And as inconvenient as it has been.

I am not grieved.

Instead, I'm happily,
face-front driving up
to the next place
I'm meant to run.

There's been a little bit of sadness.
A little bit of I can't believe where we're at now.
A whole lot of it is what it is,
as I see the dust
settle into the ground.
But that's the end of the party,
the end of the show.
Time to part ways
and see where the road
takes us each on our own.

Ships
  – Jerri Hardesty

We were
Ships
That pass in the night,
And that's not a bad thing,
Instead, we could've
Collided,
Hull crushing hull,
Bows splintered,
Leaving us both
Wrecked and sunken
On a coldswept
Ocean floor.

Friend-Zoned...Yet Again
 — *David Lange*

Relegated
I hoped this time there might be more
But I find myself, again, a friend
As I have too many times before

I should have pumped the brakes
I should have gathered in the reins
But I let a burning passion get the better of me
And now I'm suffering the pains

The pains of hopeless longings
The pains of dreams that die
The pains of self-doubt and insecurities
The pains that make me cry

I love friendships more than most
When all is said and done
But just this once, I hoped and prayed
That I had finally found the one

The one to help complete me
And with whom I might share my life
The one I might kneel down before
And ask to be my wife

I wanted her so badly
She seemed perfect in every way
I felt true affection emanating
From all she'd do and say

So why now must I rationalize
About how lucky I am to have a friend
Whilst my shattered ego staggers

DAVID LANGE

My heart mourns a lifeless end

An end to yet another lovely dream
A romantic epic left unfulfilled
A plan for a life together
Before it's birth, ignobly killed

I can't blame her, no never!
Her affection and kindness were pure and true
Banish the thought that she should have to act with malice
To prove that we were through

It's all on me, I take the blame
For building a fantasy of thin air
I must now collect the ashes
Transferred to an urn with care

Sealed tightly and placed upon the mantle
Where others rest beside
A grim reminder for the future
Of those many times I tried

Of agonies I endured and tears I shed
The painful time it took to mend
All so that I might shake a hand rather than kiss the lips
Of yet another friend

Don't get me wrong…I'm grateful
Friendship has great value, it is true
And I'll not betray the sacred trust of friendship
As true friends must swear to do

I just know there'll be those days
When an errant tear streams down my cheek
My strong will shall fortify the friendship
Though my heart occasionally grows weak

FRIEND-ZONED...YET AGAIN

I'll not abandon my dear friend
For a failure that's my own
I'll shore up the unsure timbers
Though they creak and groan

But things will never be quite right
Where heart and mind come to meet
I've passed below the archway to the Friend Zone
Engraved above, the words "You're So Sweet"

Maybe I was sweet
And maybe I was kind
But it still stings like failure
And so, I set out once more to find

That woman of my dreams
Whose company I treasure
And I hope, nay, pray this time
She'll love me in equal measure

Read Receipt
   – Kirstin Kochie

                                                          "I'm sorry"

oh shit

   "You're so brave for telling me. I appreciate and admire that. I'm sure someday someone will feel that way about you. I hope we can still be friends"

Oh. *Shit.*

Well
It could have been worse

I'll never know what was truly worse,
The rejection itself, the feeling of not being good enough
Choking on the lump in my throat as I fought to cry, to even breathe
Watching my phone screen go dark, and
Staring at my teary eyes in its reflection
Watching the girl in the black mirror watch me
And wondering
What the fuck had I *really* expected?

Or
The distance that came afterwards
The length of time it took you to text me back

                                                         Sent 2:25
                                                       Read 10:47
                                                              …

When I know you were making plans with our other friends

KIRSTIN KOCHIE

>Sent 3:30
>Read 3:32
>!

How we both hoped we could still be that much

>Sent 1:15

Or so you let me believe

>Sent 8:10
>Read: 9:25
>...

Before you

>Sent 10:34

Just

>Read 4:30

Stopped
Fucking
Trying

>Sent 6:45

No
The worst is that I still think about it
Even though we're not friends anymore, we don't even talk

>Read 11:59

READ RECEIPT

I still think about you
And sometimes it still hurts

>   Sent

It could have been worse
But that doesn't make it better, does it?

The Rented Room
– Carella Keil

Our bodies work together. If I was just flesh and lush lips and muscle and you just cock and groin and strong hands it might be good. Like machinery, all the cogs in the right place, everything sliding into its groove in just the right way at just the right moment. If. I was. Just

"Too bad I love you so much."

The topography of our friendship is made of familiar landmarks and unmarked borders to trespass. We take each other for granted. Familiarity and ease replace passion, lust. There is urgency, need. I could almost pretend. But you never caress my face, gaze into my eyes or hover above my lips for longer than an instant. I know you don't want me. But here I am, my body stretched out before you like a sandy beach. Here I am. And you don't want to make love to me. You could never make love to me. Your eyes are closed when we touch and kiss. When we…kiss. Close your eyes, I'm just a body. I'm your friend, but I am also just a body.

If it was just a mad fuck, I could do it. But our emotional terrain is barren. It's need, desperation. Desperation is a dry, endless desert. I bathe in blue salty sea water and jump out glistening wet, and a moment later, I'm parched again. Yeah I can get a fuck anywhere any time I want it. But I can't get your blue eyes on me. If you looked at me the way I needed, I would flame up like a phoenix. You have no idea what a torch I would be in bed.

That no one I've been with ever truly gave a fuck about me is a knowledge I carry secreted inside me every day. Like it matters, give it all away. Maybe if I Give and Give and Give it enough someone will fall in love with me. See past the neuroticism, see through the ugly. And I don't mind if someone falls for a fake me. Go ahead. If I could be that sparkling girl in tight black on the dance floor with the wicked smile and glistening eyes every day, I would. It's nice to fool yourself into believing you have sexual power. It's nice to think someone is attracted to a beauty you don't even know you possess. But no one's going to see beauty where there is only ugly. And I am so ugly. Not only outside but in. It's a rot that eats away at me.

A part of me is No is Yes and Yes is No. If I Push and Push and Push love will come. Yeah, like sweet juice ever came out of something rancid.

And I never give you your sexual release, and you never give me the affection, attention, passion I desire. I want to tell you the offer has expired, that I will never, ever sleep with you. I want to be cold but instead I hold on to my desperation. Desperate. Someday, I tell myself, I will be beautiful and awe-inspiring and sensual enough for you. Like your dick is the measure of my worth.

And Today, don't ever tell me I'm Beautiful again.

(An excerpt from this piece appears as the poem Thirst in Nightingale & Sparrow Issue XV: Submerged)

Push
  – Michael Artemis

I couldn't help but wait.

She said she'd have her things cleared out on Monday afternoon and asked me not to be there.

Instead of acting surprised, she walked inside and shed her coat. "It's a little dark, why don't you turn the lights on?"

"It costs too much."

Searching the kitchen cupboards, she asked me what I wanted to keep.

I shrugged and said, "mi casa es su casa."

She laughed.

It took a few minutes of picking and choosing, but she wiped away the dust off the dining table and placed two cups down – one green, one red. "Pick one," she said.

He's kissing me now. Pushing me onto the kitchen table. The floorboards are coming loose. The last rays of sun lean through the curtains.

He reaches up my shirt and my throat tightens. He pushes me by the head and I throw up on the good tablemats.

He doesn't rush to comfort me. It takes him a moment. Then he says, your panic is the sexiest part of you.

She looked at me across the table, "do you plan on choosing today?"

"What do you want me to say?"

"Something new. Something whole."

"You know I can't."

When we had our last fight, she said she couldn't live with me and the ghosts, that I had to pick her or a haunting.

"You flinch when we kiss, you know that?"

"I don't mean to."

I picked up the green cup and held it close. She left without saying goodbye.

At night when I go to take my clothes off, I look in the mirror and see her hands. I decide to leave them on.

When I dream, she shows up and pulls me into her arms. I wake up screaming.

Nothing Left
   – Debbie De Louise

There's nothing left to say.
Nothing left to do.
Nothing left to lose after losing you.

That's just the way it is.
Hard to swallow, hard to take.
Nothing left to feel.
Nothing but heartache.

I guess I should've known before.
Before I gave you my love.
Now there's nothing left to give.
It's all been given up.

And there's nothing I can say
to buy your trust.
There's nothing I can do,
even though I feel I must.

That's just the way it is.
Hard to swallow, hard to take.
Nothing left to feel.
Nothing but heartache.

I guess it's over now.
I can't follow your shadow anymore.
When my footsteps head for your door,
I have to turn the other way.

Because there's nothing left to say.
Nothing left to do.
Nothing left to lose
after losing you.

DEBBIE DE LOUISE

That's just the way it is.
Sweet at the start, bitter at the end,
like milk gone sour.
And there's nothing I can do
to change it at this hour.

I can still pretend,
But there's nothing I can do
to make your love come again.

There's nothing left to say.
Nothing left to do.
Nothing left to lose
after losing you.

Nostalgia on a Cloudy Day
  – *K.V. Raghupathi*

(in fond remembrance of mistress by her paramour)

Your pink face is like the Dianthus of the day
Your eyes like the plume of moonlit night
Your overall loveliness like the grace
of blushing morning-breaking in the skies.

And now the glorious day, the beauteous night
are like faded poppies in the evening sun of my life.
The birds that sing signal to their mates at dawn,
but to my dull ears, to my tear-blinded sight
are one with all the darkening sky, since you are miles away.

In your voice, the calling of the lapwing I noticed
like flowing music of a shepherd's flute;
and in your smile, the breaking light of Venus;
and in your quick scurrying movements
like the timid gazelle's hopping;
and in your sharp looks like the nippy eyes of a dove
searching for my loyalty in the depthless of my heart.
And all the gentle virtues in your heart
like treasured pearls in a chest.

But I miss them like the passing glow of the evening sun.
Dear, let these memories be buried memories in the dark moon.
I long for them only to realize at the end as fluffy clouds.

Questions
 –Sally Quon

great blue heron
standing alone
at the edge of the pond

i wish i could speak bird

i have a few questions, like

with all of that big, blue sky
how do you find love?

does it get very lonely
with all that empty space?

but then again,
who am i to ask?

Bookstore Haiku
   – Shai Afsai

in the poetry aisle
her cloth mask slips off –
I'm six feet away

The Boy Who Lived In the Forest
  – Sally Quon

I can still see him – long, toffee-colored hair and azure-tinted glasses, the kind John Lennon used to wear. He lived alone, off-grid, squatting on crown land, in a shack built with deadfall and cedar boughs. I longed to see it for myself, gather wood for the fire, make love on a bed of moss. He was the free spirit I could have been if life had handed me a different kind of fruit. I don't remember his name, only that he would bring me a fistful of wildflowers and grasses he gathered as he walked from forest to beach. Sometimes, he'd give me a seashell. I'd give him a pint of Guinness.

Permanent
 – Jerri Hardesty

My emotions
Fold in upon themselves,
Origami heart,
Just tug the paper tab
And the whole thing
Comes apart,
Torn open,
Laid bare,
And written on the page within --
One word --
Your name.

Loving Shadows
 – Henry Vinicio Valerio Madriz

Darkness shining in our own room,
sweating bodies complementing each other,
so, senses understanding to fulfill commands;
two that become one endless momentum:
you warm me up with the love of a mother
and I tie you up with my legs and arms.

Emotional connection becoming physical perfection,
physical perfection becoming a loving routine.

Skin smells that guide us to the meeting point:
open lower limbs longing it and for more;
an eye-before-eye kiss with a taste of honey,
not on the lips but in the smiling joint
that keeps us united under the world's door
despite our own secret isn't based on money.

Emotional connection becoming physical perfection,
physical perfection becoming a loving routine.

Darkness shining in our own way,
feeling like home with a touch or squeeze;
an anatomical rhythm that has been learned by heart,
tongue to body parts licking life and love's sway
a hearted nest that is milked by passionate bees
that seek for another encounter as a new start.

Emotional Exhibitionist
– Carella Keil

She was asking for it
wearing her heart
on her sleeve
like that.

Slut.

Phototrope
– Janis Butler Holm

I remember the sun,
torrid and insistent,
how its ruthless radiance
dazzled the eyes.
Wave after wave,
the white, obliterating heat,
searing and bleaching,
dazing each thing
to staring incandescence.

Lying here, in the dark,
I know you're not the sun.
Above me, your skin
is dusky and cool.
Your eyes are shadowed
by something in the night.
So why am I thinking
of that brutish star?
Why am I burning, burning,
burning?

...but it is not all that you make and exhibit
  – *K.V. Raghupathi*

I
I do not know how to tell what it is
but I know how to live in it.
If you may call love
but it is not all that you make and exhibit.
I cannot count the ways
as you do
but I can feel it in the depths of my soul.
When the feeling is dead and gone,
the beauty of love ends its ideal grace.

II
It comes like a cloudless night sky
with brightened stars.
By the time you realize its immensity,
it goes off like a morning sky
with the raging sun
and falls into abysmal darkness
once again!
So fleecy and elusive
yet it creates tremors in the heart
and copious tears in the eyes.
If you may call love
but it is not all that you make and exhibit.

III
Billions and billions of words in all languages
on the paper and tongue
flowed like the perennial Nile.
Without it the world is absurd
blasted in darkness with no spring.
This is a word that you cannot understand so easily.
It is thicker than blood

and thinner than gossamer;
more frequent to fail than to succeed.
Once you fall
you are sucked into the black hole,
it burns you like a wildfire.
Once you fail
you are soaked in its ashes.
If you may call love
but it is not all that you make and exhibit.

IV
It isn't a universal virtue that
many religious heads parrot.
The more you talk about it,
the more you become foolish about yourself.
It is like a lone house on the hill
where you venture to stay
make soup out of your dreams
drink and sing songs
until the morning sunshine shatters.
If you may call love
but it is not all that you make and exhibit.

V
It is neither sweet nor bitter
neither cold nor warm
neither hard nor soft
but when it touches
it burns you in a fire.
Out of the season
it comes like a silent breeze
and ends in a violent wind
for no reason.
If you may call love
but it is not all that you make and exhibit.

VI

With it, nothing is harder
without it, nothing is softer;
About it, there isn't anything
that I would want to know
because it weighs the world
on its four letters
and crumbles on four letters
HATE.
If you may call love
but it is not all that you make and exhibit.

VII
I miss the world when you are beside me
I miss you when the world is before me
It is miserable even if once I don't fall in
I will have blemishes, I will carry scars.
I may be tarnished, tainted and decorated
with filth; yet if once I don't fall in
at least with my body…
that is where the romance begins in love's landscape.
If you may call love
but it is not all that you make and exhibit.

VIII
When you love the LOVE,
you mistake it for a woman,
you feel its warmth,
you hold it to your heart,
you think a thousand crimson roses
tickling your skin and you feel safe,
you float in a perfumed lake
and dream about castles.
Until you are free from all that you make and exhibit
you are never free to feel what it is!

Don't Ever Think…
   – Carol Alena Aronoff

It's when you're in despair
that someone throws you a double
negative: *Don't ever think
that I don't love you.*
You write the words down,
make sure you've got 'em right;
still they don't sink in.
You say them over and over,
looking for hidden meaning,
a secret tunnel leading
straight to his heart.

Think back to other
conversations,
try to remember exactly
what was said.
Is it just insecurity
that binds you to the dried
wood of old words?
What will it finally take--for you
to believe someone can love
you, that he means
just what he says?

You torture yourself a few more
hours, forgetting flights
into emptiness and bliss,
sweet words sinking
into sated flesh. And then,
on the edge of sleep, or madness--
you're not sure which--
you recall one kiss,

CAROL ALENA ARONOFF

one moment
when all thought stopped--
and you knew.

Fool's Gold
  —Myna Wallin

Her kitchen was immaculate,
outfitted with state-of-the-art appliances—
part of the settlement from husband no. 1.

It was easier this way, to serve
herself up as a plausible chef,
and ensnare another husband.

She faked so much of it—
especially the cooking.
Her bedroom was encrusted

with mirrors, giving the impression
of sensual delights yet to come.
In truth, she needed to consume

her reflection from every angle possible
since she demanded of herself
sartorial perfection.

Soaking wet when the doorbell rang,
she enfolded herself in a luxurious towel
and nothing else. It was a hoary ploy

she'd seen in a film with Monroe or
Betty Grable. She acted flustered even
though she wasn't.

The caramelized ham was on low
in the convection oven—
the sizzling scent of it

mixing with her perfume, an intoxicating

odour suggesting both homemaker and vixen.
She was a lapsed vegetarian—

the aroma of meat excited her
now, in a way she couldn't explain.
Her online man about to walk through

her front door, he'd have to match
the stencil she had constructed.
There was no room for adjustments.

Her pheromones were a satellite
picking up eligible men in the area.
It never occurred to her

she was enough on her own
before adding these concocted layers.
Feeling inadequate, aspiring to live a life

others envied, propping herself up on the arm
of a wealthy man—
no pyrite: she required 19 carat gold

around her left ring finger
before she'd feel at ease again.
Before she could live glamorously.

Otherwise, she drank too much
and went salsa dancing, lowering
her standards on a Saturday night.

Published in *Anatomy of An Injury* (Inanna Publications, 2018)

Teddy Bear Love
 – Michael Artemis

In that way a heart loved its host, or a stomach lusted for food, or an autopsy needed a stern older gent with yellowing fingers to look over the paperwork. It was textbook tragedy: she was the woman who had it all, Othello's disciple, one who loved well but not too wisely, and he was her Desdemona, her light, her climax, her siren song. Maybe she mistook comfort for the button eyes, waiting for idle touches, stuffed with epithets of lost loves and mistakes made. There were no complications or worries with men like him. He would never pull the threads. His happiness was stitched to his face. All she knew is that she loved him, because who wouldn't love him?

Ten Years
– Lisa Diaz Meyer

It was ten years ago,
I knew I'd never visit you again.
It was ten years ago,
I knew we'd never speak again.
It was ten years ago,
We'd never laugh together,
Or dance together, cry together,
Pray this nightmare
Wasn't real together.
Ten years ago,
Life had a death sentence.
And it was ten years ago,
There was an end of the world.

Road Trips
   – Carella Keil

Enough tears to float your way to Wonderland
Not enough poppies to forget it all

Cut the thorns off every rose; still your fingers
Bleed

He only sees you
Through the broken Looking-Glass
It cuts his eyes
So now he won't look at all

You sew shadows to the tips of his toes
Follow him wherever he goes
Not enough fairy dust to make you fly
Fall asleep with a bloody nose

Water only makes you dirtier
Not enough kisses to wake you up

Her glass slipper on his windowsill
Stale breadcrumbs leading home

He gives you a key, but you lock yourself

Out.

   (Originally Published in Dipity No. 1: Human Typewriters from Around the World)

Choice
    – Leslie Arambula

half broken
on a smoky night,
he split himself.
shame

sprayed out of him,
drenching her in ichor,
burning like a flame
she did not wipe away.

instead
she stitched up his wound,
even as the droplets dug
and marred her skin

he walked
away
whole
and

she
sat
forced
to endure

a golden leaf
floating to the ground,
a brown dandelion,
crunched into concrete

a final shred of light
casting the world into darkness,

LESLIE ARAMBULA

a shout echoing
off of empty, hollow walls

Heartbreaker
 – Jerri Hardesty

He took her into his heart,
Invited her to join him.
He made promises to her
Of true love,
Of happiness,
Of forever.

He took her into his life,
Taught her to love him,
Convinced her to trust him,
Molded her desires
To his whims.

He took her into his house,
Broke all her defenses,
Shook up her life
And severed her ties,
Owned her completely --
And concluded
His experiment.

He poured her under his door
Out into the rain.

without you
 – Candice Louisa Daquin

your betrayal came before the post on monday
if I listened it may have sounded
like paper in air, losing gravity
the unexpected slap of shiny magazine
and echoing hinged snap of closed-door flap
the postman left his shoe imprints in snow
one way in, one way out and the bare branches of the trees
were cold dancers cupping themselves to imaginary furnace
you had already gone before the skies admitted
their talcum-powdered descent of white
your letter, handwriting in your bold certain shape
the same hand that had led me up the stairs
a silver bracelet bought when we visited the seaside, on your wrist
strong hand, reaching for me, for my rustle and my yawning silhouette
we were shapes against the mirror of moonlight
streaming our own version of whispers and little cries
you never let go of my hand even
as you turned your neck and slept, dreamlessly by my side
and I lay in partial light feeling your resonance
play like an instrument on my damp skin
your upright, careful letter and the last word, your name
a name I had put into the core of me and melted down
covering any fear that you'd crack my heart
open like a woodland walnut and expose the soft innards
no, not this woman, with her fingers reading my brail
and her tongue searching for stars in the folds of hesitate
she has breathed me in, carved her name in my wood
I cannot stir without a part of her moving alongside me
life no longer singular I am now and always, illuminated
by her rounding glow and the peach dream of her thighs
wrapped in mutual surround, the open window
carrying our symphony into gloaming night wind
how then are you gone?

as rapid as my chest threatens to explode
a single firework
removed from me and behind, spending in your wake
emptiness
letters furthering no explanation, blurring in porcelain horror
if I had listened
maybe the stir of settling snow or else
some torn part would reveal, the sense in loss
I stand by the picture window
wearing an old shirt of yours
yellow at the collar and faded with wash
across the road, a neighbor walks her dogs
she glances my way and sees
only the shadow of
a life without
you.

When You Took Away Your Love
   – Debbie De Louise

You don't know what you took from me
when you took away your love.
You took away the summer days.
You took away the sun and flowers,
the music, and my happiest hours.
You took away everything from me
when you took away your love.

You don't know how you broke my heart
when you took away your love.
You took away the winter afternoons,
and all my holiday cheer,
the bright feeling whenever you were near.
But you don't care
that you took everything away from me
when you took away your love.

You don't know how I felt
when you took away your love.
Because if you did, it would never have been done.
You took away everything I ever wanted.

You took away my dreams and hopes,
the wonder of the wind, the magic in the rain.
Now nothing is the same
because you took away my heart,
left just a little part,
the part that feels the pain.
Oh, but what I wouldn't do to have you back again.

It's a fact
that remains so true.

DEBBIE DE LOUISE

That there's no going back
when someone takes away their love,
takes away their love from you.

Erasure Poem
   – Carella Keil

He took my words and left
The empty page
Instead

I'm just his intermission but
He's the whole damn play

Broken
   – Sally Quon

You took me –
raw and fresh –
wore me down,
broke me open.

You taught me lessons.

Taught them again
when it didn't work the first time.

You molded me
into the person I am today.
Look at me now.

Look, I said.

Are you proud of your work?

Heartbreak Aisle
   – *Carella Keil*

Eat a dream
Suck my face
Your darkness is pulling you away from me

One night blurs into another, a fine blue powder
I won't hold down my heart
But I don't hold up my head

Stars streak across the sky
I tell you
There are more memories of him I've forgotten
Than I can count

Full moon floating over the subway ride home
What kind of dream are you

The kind that leaves rashes on the mind.

Put out your cigarette
On the painting of my face

Take a walk down the Heartbreak Aisle

How far
Until the sink reaches your knees
How long
Until the fall reaches your heart.

Self-portrait of an Art Gallery
And the third page of goodbye
In your loose-leaf paper heart

CARELLA KEIL

It's over so
You can hang up the Sun
On the tired hook on your wall

(Originally published by Troublemaker Firestarter Vol. 3)

Evasion
   – BA Brittingham

Why is it so difficult to write of you
when I have effortlessly scrawled about the
spouse abandoned long ago — not because he didn't
love me, but because he loved the bottle more —
or of the sweet and subdued young man who
chose to bow out by his own hand?

They say that summoning the words we'd like to use
to exorcize those who've wounded us, bestows
on them the balm to erase the wrath and distress,
thus keeping our words more compassionate.
I'm not sure I believe that since it has been
twenty-five years and still I feel the bitterness of
bile rising in my throat.

They say, "forgive and forget" and though
I got around to absolving you after a decade
separated us from your betrayal, the anguish
and the scorch from that shock remains
as fresh as the vermilion tulips I cut this morning.

I did not cry for days or weeks, or even months,
I cried for years. I could not understand why,
When I had so often forgiven your frequent and
childish mistakes, you were unwilling to excuse
whatever you thought me guilty of.

Perhaps this is how God or Fate or Destiny
chooses to replace the pain of eventual spousal death:
by making us suffer moderately over a long period
rather than the jolt of all-at-once. Is one actually better
then the other? I'm still guessing — but I doubt it.

Another Chance
— Shai Afsai

(Inspired by Gilbert Alfred Franklin's sculpture Orpheus Ascending*)*

Soundlessly, Hermes and Eurydice return to Hades
across from RISD Museum.
Orpheus, naked and aghast,
left hand gripping his lyre,
gasps in open-mouthed horror
as she departs
and he loses her a second time.
They move in bronze
on Benefit St.,
atop a sloping palm frond fountain.
For the entrance to the underworld
is in Providence,
near a place Lovecraft, forlorn,
wandered shivering at night,
not far from the granite Athenaeum library
where Poe courted the poet Sarah Helen Whitman
and borrowed *Stanley: Or, Recollections of a Man of the World*.
In the capital of the smallest state
lies passage to the abode of those
who have passed from this world.
If one walks in the cold
between midnight and dawn,
it is still possible to stand lonesome in that spot,
to watch the three faintly lit figures move,
and to remember:
bad things happen when we look back.

Callous
– BA Brittingham

Oh, there were many nights and days
when I thought of you and was pinioned
against the past by excruciating pain:
midnights when I would dream garishly
of the one for whom you left me; days of
prolonged sunlight when suddenly your
laughing face would intrude upon those
brief golden moments which had been blissfully
vacant of your memory; when I was out serenely
image-capturing and would recall a similar locale
from years before when we had viewed
something and then laughed together.

Always the terrible twist of torture; the remembrance,
always following, obstructing my breath, my heart,
never letting me be at peace.

And I prayed for something grander, stronger, kinder
that might free me from incessant agony. Tried to\
tell myself you were dead, and by being so I could
finally gain release. Yet still it resided within,
like road rash on every single internal organ; like a
spreading sepsis that refused to liberate me until demise.

Then one day, when fifteen years had passed I
fathomed that you had slipped into my thoughts
and there were no stinging sobs, no phenomenal pain;
that there was nothing but a vacuum, a numbed and hollow place.

I once shook hands with a master woodworker, his
fingers so hardened by years of cutting and carving
that it was like holding a warm leather glove. Realized

that at last something splendid had found me, had insulated the hurt
by forming a great callous above the
tough-skinned tomb where your remembrance dwelt.

And I thought: *finally! Freedom!*

Now all that is left to do is create a duplicate
– to shelter my heart.

Dear Mistakes
   – Mary C. M. Phillips

Dear Mistakes,

I didn't like you the first time we met, and nothing has changed.

Please stop visiting me whenever you feel like it and reminding me that you exist, as you've become boring and frankly…predictable.

Everyone needs to reinvent themselves at some point and that goes for you too. Here's an idea: wear a costume henceforth. Maybe a costume in the form of a lesson. Yes, that's it, dress like a lesson! That would look good on you!

In fact, the next time you visit, I will make sure to only open the door if you're wearing your new "lesson" costume. Otherwise…you can't come in.

This is my house and these are my rules.

Your former hostess,

Mary

Past Lives
  – Dion O'Reilly

If I say when I met you, I saw atoms
that were once part of someone else
whom I'd loved the way a beaten child
        loves a small white rat,

I do not mean to suggest that you were
not possessed of an attractive scent.
Hint of burnt leaves. Tomato sweat.
        Reek of a car crash.

What is it about accidents
that rushes the blood
into the chambers of the heart?
        The way every neighbor gathers

to watch a mansion flame.
The urge to witness
a jet, aloof and unreachable,
        plunge like a comet.

I rubbernecked my own demise,
watched myself walk with rocks
in my pocket along your tideline.
        Your eyes,

flat as that concrete cast
of slick sand, an unperturbed sheen
that swallowed itself. By which I mean,
        I loved the look of you,

DION O'REILLY

vaporous in the way of a mirage
that wanted to be water.
Did you love me
      for my thirst?

Even now, I cup the air,
lift nothing to my lips.

"Past Lives" was previously published in *Spillway*.

And so Catherine Howard practiced laying her head on the block, to try the face she would pull when the axe fell, or perhaps to simulate a sleepless night
  – Michael Artemis

A body is an effigy
A glass model   a Dorian Grey
You peel back another layer   there's no worship in words
The pillows didn't protect me   (the pillows are all I have left)
He stands over my bed some nights
Paper cracks in my skin   eyes that never quite meet his
A stare that's dead   a laugh that's cold
The bedframe held me upright   (the bedframe is all I have left)
Fire crackle, toppled over
He stands over my bed some nights
                         He stands
                         He stands
Lie back and think of England (England is all I have left)
                         He stood

(but then again)

ah, yes;
i know i am evil
for not being the girl
you dreamed of and instead
being real—

ah, yes;
i know i am evil for being
a strong woman instead of
your damsel in distress
arm candy—

but you're not evil for intentionally
leading me on,
for making me think you cared
about me when you had no intention to;

you're not evil for crushing me
beneath the weight of all your lust and
marrying the woman you cheated on me with—

if you're coming to burn the witch,
then i must warn you i've always been burning
for i am a phoenix hearted woman and
my tears and flowers can save you but my fires
will destroy you if you step too close;
and i consider you an enemy so i would keep your distance
if i were you (but then again if i were you i wouldn't be such an ass).

-*linda m. crate*

Ghost In My Rearview Mirror
  – Melody Lipford

Dear You,

I'm done, sitting here.
Thinking, wishing that you'd appear.
Now, you're just a shadow,
that's distant–
reminiscent of something great,
that was never here.

And after all this, we got so close,
but fear took you into overdrive.

And now,
you're just like a ghost in my rearview mirror.

Senryu (To the Curb)
 – Jerri Hardesty

She always complained
He never took out the trash --
That's where they found him.

Sorry, Not Sorry
   – Sally Quon

I'm sorry
but I don't think I have

anything

to apologize for.
It was you

who raised your hand,
a surprise in the night
so often I stopped sleeping

naked, because

it made me more vulnerable.
It was you

whose tongue cut, with
edges like slips of shale,

the bite of a whip,
bringing me to my knees.

It was you
who undermined every move,
countered every effort,

like a strategic game of Risk
you didn't need to win

as long as I was the loser.

i will never thank you

there's a lot of things
i resent about you,
like the fact you married
the woman you cheated on me
with or the fact you were so
happy that i wasn't pregnant when we were
at the clinic and i had to pretend it was my
period when i had really had a miscarriage so
kudos to all of your sensitivity there;

i resent that you were simply looking for a
good time instead of a life partner
and that you used your lust a weapon to destroy
who i was so i had to begin again anew;

i reclaimed my voice and my power and i refound
my magic but i will never thank you—

that happened because i decided to be
stronger than the pain you gave me which was
dragging me into a deeper depression than what i even
had in high school,

i had done so well then you undid all the progress i did;
and for that i resent you, too—

you have no idea how hard i had to work to become okay again.

-linda m. crate

I Sit Inside Dusk
   – Carella Keil

I sit inside dusk
like a cozy chair
kick my shoes off
drink scalding cup after cup of tea
feel my ribs scream for food

This denial feels great
I've never denied myself anything before
I seldom deny anyone anything

I love the way the trees scratch the sky
I love the way they beg for their leaves back
I love the cars driving endlessly, flames
on a road
Ceasing at the corner of my window
where dusk steals everything

I'm learning that everything ceases
where I begin
and where I end, there are only ashes

I'm learning about things that mean something
and things that mean nothing
I'm learning that the paper swan on my bedside table
unfolds like a rose, every petal
poignant with promise

I'm learning that all of your kisses crumble in my palms
I'm learning
the ashes I carry in my heart

are mine, not yours.

I walk through life and watch dust fall from my fingertips
I'd love to touch your pretty face
but worry what I might do to the thought of you

So I dream on it.

I love this denial
the shadow of trees
falling across my face
The damn phone that won't stop ringing
the leak in the bathtub faucet

This gray sunset
lasts for weeks

I love the joke that this is all normal.
I love lying in bed with the lover I know best
His arms are always open to embrace me
he loves sinking deep down inside me.
He's never truly gone
even when I'm with someone else.

I love this denial and the hot tea
that makes my lips crack
Only depression loves a girl like this
it's a bed for one but he fits inside me
snugly

I SIT INSIDE DUSK

And when he whispers in my ear,
it's always "Ashes, ashes, dust"
And I begin to forget
I ever had embers in my eyes
and flames beneath my skin.

He's not a jealous lover. He's a constant.
He tells me it doesn't matter how hard I burn
he'll always be here for me
waiting for me, in a bed of my own ashes.

So I turn inside myself and sleep
and hope never to awake.

(Originally published by Sunday Mornings at the River Winter 2022)

a wolf without protection

they say i should wish you well,
but instead i am wishing you
every hell you've ever given me and
anyone else who is guilty of the crime
of loving you;

they say to bury the hatchet but i would
rather bury you like you did me in your
avalanche of lust—

they say i should hide my crazy,
but i have done that for years and sometimes
people just need to know that you're
done being a doormat;

so don't think you'll be stepping all over me—

i have rediscovered my magic,
reclaimed my voice and my power;

but i believe that wicked people should be
punished and so i hope everything you shattered in me
will come back to visit you and remember you
can't pray to the moon because she's my mother so
you're a wolf without protection.

-linda m. crate

The House of Echoes
 – *N.E Salmon*

I live in a house of echoes
Every marred plate and chipped bowl painful reverberations
The mocking utensils cackling as they scrape lonely porcelain.
The walls are painted glass
Stained colours and harsh mixes coalescing into veneers of memory
The unseen cracks now so clear
A broken mirror, warped and twisted, awful in its reflection
My reflection. Our reflection.
The cackling chairs and the boastful table crowd me mockingly
Couples and pairs, waiting on the next meal, wondering what's for dinner.
Petty squabbles, both more grandiose and meaningful in their meaninglessness
the more they bounce against the home's empty corners.
I sleep in a bed of hollows, the mattresses yawning chasm
Shaped in half remembered groves where you once lay

My feet are frozen as I stare at the memories written in the bricks
The foundations turned to sand as the walls seep to the floor
Lying in ruined puddles on the ground where once reflected happiness.
The piled dunes of arguments and merriments erode with every passing day.
Where once a hopeful ocean yawned at my feet nothing but a blackened void calls to me
I try to shout back but my throat it drowning in helpless thoughts
Bubbling at the corners of my mouth in inky froth,
My pathetic hands writing messages never sent,
Begging for its darkness to cover my heart.

As it claws at my neck I wonder if it was all worth it.
As it smothers my chest I realise that it couldn't be.
It beats for a moment.

N.E SALMON

A sad and pitiful thing, full of hopes and weezing regrets
As it buckles my knees I see it for what it truly is
As it envelops me like a charred blanket, as quickly as it came, it pulls away.

On the dusted ocean I am left trembling
Remembering it now as though it hadn't happened to me
The body we had once shared had been torn apart, stretched thin
so thinly pulled that the body is no longer here
Yet at least I no longer see the paint shattered windows
No longer do the sounds of my own footsteps follow me
Like a Web shattering, there's enough left of that hollow shell which held me all along
There's enough of me to keep the echoes inside.

After All This Time
 – Michelle Chermaine Ramos

If only my younger self could see us now.
I never imagined this time would come.

Us. Like this.

Reminiscing over some dinner and wine,
the fine humming of the violin in the air
mingling with our laughter.

And I can't help but stare into your eyes
and recognize the same familiar glimmer
that hypnotized me years ago.

But tonight, that is no longer so.

You crack a joke
and I chuckle inside
realizing how,
when what seemed like a lifetime ago,
the sound of your voice
would make my heart sing.

But now,
nothing rings.
Nothing has for a long time.

It's as if another version of me
must have loved another version of you
in some other distant dimension
of a strange multiverse
in the Twilight Zone.

How comforting this is to know

MICHELLE CHERMAINE RAMOS

that *we* are now ghosts.

It's amazing how some things
always stay the same,
as it's magically liberating
how some don't.

Your love is here.

That place is no longer my place.
Your heart is no longer mine,
as mine is no longer yours.
That door has been closed
for some time now.

Time has faithfully sewn old wounds
and cured us sooner
than I ever believed it could.
Oh, how much we have grown!

My heart overflows seeing
that things are as they're meant to be.
The distance between us now
the same as your love sitting in front of me.
And I'm happy you've chosen wisely.

As I share a slice of cake with your soulmate,
we chat excitedly all night
about love,
life,
and everything in between.
I marvel at how we relate over how much
we appreciate the same things.

Then it struck me.

How,

AFTER ALL THIS TIME

for those hours,
I forgot that *you* were even right there.

How do you measure this miracle?

Once upon a time,
when you and I ended,
it felt like I would never mend.

And now,
each time I see you both very much in love,
my heart swells above all measure
treasuring how lucky I am
to be doubly blessed with such good friends.

Regrets
  – Anna Sanderson

My list of regrets
Is a blank page

It is the space
Between us
that nobody sees

The unspoken words
Caught in my throat
That make it hard to breathe

It is everything
that's empty now
Like promises and drawers
And your side of the bed

And that hollow
In the pit of my stomach
That still calls out to you

Maybe regrets are always
Written with invisible ink
But things unseen
Are just as real
As others
Memories. Love. Air.

You are all these things to me.

And I am sorry.

now i am grateful

once upon a time
i cried,
begging you to love me;

now i am grateful
you set me free—

wouldn't want to stand
in the shadow of a man
without a heart or integrity,

and i know one day someone
will cut you down to the bone
in a way that hurts more than
you cut me and if the universe
is feeling generous perhaps i'll get
to see with a glass of champagne in hand;

but it's okay if i don't—just knowing
one day the fires of your lust will be used
against you is enough for me.

-linda m. crate

Closure
  – Carol Alena Aronoff

It was a place she'd been before.
She knew its folded pockets
like she knew the contours of her face.

It was a brave place, this alley housing
fools and phantoms, dumpsters filled
with burning news and the unrecycled

refuse of a privileged life. She had waited
here on starless nights when hope
was still unshuttered and her love,

a window of mullioned glass. She had waited
until a cold dawn claimed her right to linger
and she faded back into living shadow.

And now she had returned, clad in clouds
and cotton wool, a shawl of memory
careless about her shoulders.

She had found life without him, a bed sitting
room with frayed sofa, a few books, gray cat.
Still, a ribbon of curiosity remained.

She would wait in that backlit alley
until his silhouette, once majestic,
now stooped with age and diminished,

filled the unshaded window of her dreams.
She watched until she saw he was alone--still--
then waited as he turned out the light.

Woken, Not Broken
  – *Michelle Chermaine Ramos*

You thought you had broken me
the last time we spoke.

You walked out the door
expecting me to implore you
to please,
please
come back.

As if my lack of a reaction
over the way you acted
after you unfriended and blocked me
meant that you had won that argument.

You thought the silent treatment
was a power move.

Ooh…
how fun was it
when it proved to be wrong
as soon as you turned right around
and threw a fit
furiously knocking,
demanding to be let back in.

As if *you*
had the right
to decide when you can
just waltz in and out of my life.

As if unblocking me
and insisting on re-opening that door
should automatically

restore things to the way they were before.

Oh…but that door is locked now!

Never have I ever
brought the trash back in
—especially
after it has so conveniently taken itself out.

Let that fact sink into your head.

I'm not broken—*but I have woken*
—and am way, way wiser instead.

And I have you to thank for it.

ABOUT THE AUTHORS

SHAI AFSAI

Shai Afsai lives in Providence, Rhode Island. Enough said.

LESLIE ARAMBULA

Leslie Arambula is a teacher, writer, and freelance world builder. She writes poetry, short stories, video game adventures, and everything in between.

CAROL ALENA ARONOFF

Carol Alena Aronoff, Ph.D. is a psychologist, teacher and poet. Her work has appeared in numerous journals and anthologies and won several prizes. She was twice nominated for a Pushcart Prize. Carol has published 4 chapbooks (Cornsilk, Tapestry of Secrets, Going Nowhere in the Time of Corona, A Time to Listen) and 6 full-length poetry collections: The Nature of Music, Cornsilk, Her Soup Made the Moon Weep, Blessings From an Unseen World, Dreaming Earth's Body (with artist Betsie Miller-Kusz) as well as The Gift of Not Finding: Poems for Meditation. Currently, she resides in rural Hawaii.

MICHAEL ARTEMIS

Michael Artemis is a queer short story and poetry writer born in Derbyshire, England. They have a passion for writing horror and are currently working on their Master's in Creative Writing at Edge Hill University. They also collect mugs.

B. A. BRITTINGHAM

Born and raised in the grittiness of New York City, Brittingham spent a large segment of her adult years in the blue skies and humidity of South Florida. Today she resides along the magnificent (and sometimes tumultuous) shores of Lake Michigan.

Her essays have appeared in the Hartford Courant and Litgleam Magazine; short stories in Florida Literary Foundation's hardcover anthology, Paradise; in the 1996 Florida First Coast Writers' Festival, and in Britain's World Wide Writers "The Note in the Wood," was a semi-finalist in the 2003 Nelson Algren Awards and was published in the June 2008 issue of Shore Magazine. Recently published in Anthology of Short Stories-Autumn 2021 was "Loose Ends."

Poetry has appeared in Kitchen Sink Magazine, the ocean waves, Words for the Earth, the Crone's Words, Green Shoe Sanctuary, and Halcyon Days.

LINDA M. CRATE

Linda M. Crate (she/her) is a Pennsylvanian writer. Her works have been published in numerous magazines and anthologies both online and in print. She is the author of eleven poetry chapbooks, the latest being: fat & pretty (dancing girl press, June 2022). She's also the author of the novella Mates (Alien Buddha Publishing, March 2022). She has four micro-poetry collections out. She has published four full-length poetry collections Vampire Daughter (Dark Gatekeeper Gaming, February 2020), The Sweetest Blood (Cyberwit, February 2020), Mythology of My Bones (Cyberwit, August 2020), and you will not control me (Cyberwit, March 2021).

CANDICE LOUISA DAQUIN

Candice Louisa Daquin works as Senior Editor for Indie Blu(e) Publishing, a feminist micro-press, and is the co-editor of two award-winning anthologies; SMITTEN this is what love looks like (lesbian poetry) and The Kali Project (Indian women writing poetry). Daquin is also Poetry Editor for Parcham Literary Magazine and The Pine Cone Review. She is Editorial Partner for Blackbird Press and Writer-in-Residence with Borderless Journal. Daquin edits stand-alone poetry and prose as well as working part-time as a Psychotherapist, specializing in childhood sexual abuse. Her latest book Tainted by the Same Counterfeit is published by Finishing Line Press. Her first novel The Cruelty, is due out in 2023.

JERRI HARDESTY

Jerri Hardesty lives in the woods of Alabama with husband, Kirk, also a poet. They run the nonprofit poetry organization, New Dawn Unlimited, Inc. (NewDawnUnlimited.com) Jerri has had over 500 poems published and has won almost 2000 awards and titles in both written and spoken word/performance poetry.

JANIS BUTLER HOLM

Janis Butler Holm served as Associate Editor for *Wide Angle*, the film journal, and currently works as a writer and editor in sunny Los Angeles. Her prose, poems, and performance pieces have appeared in small-press, national, and international magazines. Her plays have been produced in the U.S., Canada, Russia, and the U.K.

DEBBIE DE LOUISE

Debbie De Louise is a reference librarian at a public library. She's the author of 14 novels including the six books of the Cobble Cove cozy mystery series featuring Alicia the librarian and Sneaky, the library cat, and the new Buttercup Bend cozy mysteries featuring Cathy Carter, the owner of a pet cemetery and rescue center. Debbie's other books include standalone mysteries, a paranormal romance, a time-travel novel, and a collection of cat poems. She also writes articles for Catster.com and has published dozens of short stories and poems in anthologies. She's a member of the Cat Writers' Association, Sisters-in-Crime, International Thriller Writers, and the Long Island Authors

Group. She lives on Long Island with her husband, daughter, and two cats. Learn more about her and her books by visiting https://debbiedelouise.com.

CARELLA KEIL

"I wasn't the kind of person who was afraid to show her scars. I saw beauty and strength in survival. Now I see survival, strength, beauty. And scars." Carella is a poet and digital artist who splits her time between the ethereal world of dreams, and Toronto, Canada, depending on the weather. Recently, her writing has appeared in Columbia Journal, Myth & Lore, Solstice Literary Magazine, Deep Overstock, Paddler Press, Nightingale & Sparrow, Querencia Press, Stripes Literary Magazine, Writeresque, Superlative Literary Journal, Free Verse Revolution and Boats Against the Current. Forthcoming publications include Door is a Jar, Grub Street, Sunday Mornings at the River, Musing Publications, Sheepshead Review, MONO and Troublemaker Firestarter.

    instagram.com/catalogue.of.dreams
    twitter.com/catalogofdream

KIRSTIN KOCHIE

Kirstin Kochie is a poetry and fiction writer from Long Island and recent graduate of Hofstra University's English department and Publishing Studies program. During her tenure at Hofstra, she joined the English Society worked with fellow English majors and writing enthusiasts to produce the group's literary magazine, Font. Kirstin was also invited to join academic honor society Phi Beta Kappa as a graduating student in 2020. Her work has been previously published in Font and by Phi Beta Kappa as the runner up of the 2021 Recent Graduate Essay Contest. This is her first publication with Red Penguin.

DAVID LANGE

David Lange was born and grew up on Long Island, New York. A graduate of the United States Air Force Academy, he served for 30 years as an Active Duty officer in the United States Air Force before retiring in 2018. Colonel Lange is a decorated combat veteran and flew numerous combat, combat support, and humanitarian relief missions during his career. He was awarded the prestigious Institute of Navigation Superior Achievement Award in recognition of his life-long accomplishments as a practicing navigator. David loves sharing stories of hope and inspiration. He has numerous short stories, essays, and poems published within various anthologies and his memoir, "Quest: My Journey Through La Mancha," was published in 2020.

MELODY LIPFORD

Melody Lipford is a poet and author based in southwest Virginia writing on various subjects from the Appalachian region to her Christian faith. Previous publications include her debut poetry collection entitled Diary of Psalms, "Nanny's Kitchen" Train River Poetry: Winter 2020 Anthology, and "Guiding Star" Calla Press Magazine, among others. Follow Melody on Facebook and Instagram @melodylipfordpoetry or her website at melodylipfordpoetry.wordpress.com for more content and updates on her upcoming debut devotional.

MATT MARTINEK

Matt Martinek is a singer/songwriter and dark fiction author from Johnstown, PA, whose passion is the creative process itself. Whether it's through song or the written word, Matt's works always find their audience. His writing credits include short stories for Sirens Call Publications, Hellbound Books, Savage Realms Gamebooks, and Coffin Bell Journal, amongst many others. Matt has also recently published his first collection of dark fiction stories, What Evil Lurks..., as well as his newest horror project, The Oddest Couple: The Collected Edition.

HENRY VINICIO VALERIO MADRIZ

Born in Atenas, Costa Rica, in 1969, the author is a teacher who studied and graduated in English Teaching, and Linguistics and Literature. He also enjoys drawing and painting and outdoor activities. He has taught English and Spanish (in the USA as well), as foreign languages, for almost 30 years; he is currently working for the Ministry of Public Education, at a bilingual public high school, in San Carlos, Costa Rica. He has published poems and short stories in several online magazines. He is the author of "Strange Fate" (short story), Darkness Falls (anthology), The Red Penguin Collection, USA, and "Running" (short story), Strangest Fiction Anthology Volume One, USA. The author got shortlisted (top 10) for the North American Continent in Voice of Peace: 1st Intercontinental Poetry And Short Story Anthology 2021, The League of Poets.

LISA DIAZ MEYER

Lisa Diaz Meyer is the author of the award-winning dark fiction short stories/dark poetry series, The All Roads Collection. Her works are also featured in several Red Penguin anthologies as well as Nassau County Poetry and Bards Annual publications. Born and raised in Brooklyn, N.Y., she now hails from Long Island's south shore. Visit lisadiazmeyer.com for more info.

DION O'REILLY

Dion O'Reilly's debut collection, Ghost Dogs, was runner-up for The Catamaran Prize and shortlisted for The Eric Hoffer Award. Her second book Sadness of the Apex Predator will be published by University of Wisconsin's Cornerstone Press in 2024. Her work appears in The Sun, Rattle, Cincinnati Review, Narrative, The Slowdown, and elsewhere. She facilitates private workshops, hosts a podcast at The Hive Poetry Collective, and is a reader for Catamaran Literary Quarterly. Most recently, her poem "The Value of Tears" was chosen by the poet Denise Duhamel as winner of the Glitter Bomb Award.

MARY C. M. PHILLIPS

Mary C. M. Phillips is a caffeinated wife, mother, writer and musician. Her inspirational essays have been published in numerous bestselling anthologies. Her spoken-word poetry is available on iTunes and streaming platforms such as Spotify. Follow her @marycmphil on Twitter.

SALLY QUON

Sally Quon is a dirt-road diva and teller of tales, living in the Okanagan. She has been shortlisted for Vallum Magazine's Chapbook Prize two consecutive years and is an associate member of the League of Canadian Poets. Her work has been published in numerous anthologies including Chicken Soup for the Soul—the Forgiveness Fix, BIG, Straightening Her Crown, and Worth More Standing. Her personal blog, https://featherstone-creative.com is where she posts her backcountry adventures and photos.

K.V. RAGHUPATHI

Poet, short story writer, novelist, book reviewer, and critic, K.V. Raghupathi, though he was born in a Telugu-speaking family in Andhra Pradesh, India writes in English. His poetry is widely anthologized and published in journals. He began writing seriously in the 1980s and has so far published thirteen poetry collections that include Desert Blooms (1987), Echoes Silent (1988), The Images of a Growing Dying City (1989), Small reflections (2000), Samarpana (2006), Voice of the Valley (2006, 2014), Wisdom of the Peepal Tree (2006, 2014) Dispersed Symphonies (2010), Orphan and Other Poems (2010), Between Me and the Babe (2014), On and Beyond the Surface (2018), The Mountain is Calling… (2018), and Transition (2022). He is well-known for his mystical poetry. His poetry is endowed with rich philosophy, mystical/transcendental thoughts, romantic elements, and dense imagery comprising similes, metaphors, personifications, apostrophes, irony, climax, anti-climax, and full of rhetoric and symbols. Besides, he occasionally writes on social and political subjects with empathy and sympathy. A former academic, he has settled quietly in Tirupati, India, and can be reached at his mailing: drkvraghupathi9@gmail.com

MICHELLE CHERMAINE RAMOS

Michelle Chermaine Ramos (www.michellechermaine.com) is a multi-disciplinary artist, writer, and journalist in Toronto, Canada. Raised in the U.A.E and of Filipino, Spanish, and Japanese descent, her visual art and words weave different cultural threads to reveal magic in everyday life.
  Twitter: @ChelleChermaine
  Instagram: @michellechermaine
  Facebook: http://www.facebook.com/MichelleChermaineArt/

N.E. SALMON

NE Salmon is a London born writer whose main skill is being able to fall asleep in any and every situation, when he is not napping he is irregularly updating his blog at thesalmonmuse.wordpress.com and debating the causes and consequences of fantasy plot points with himself and increasingly worried Wife and Baby Daughter.

ANNA SANDERSON

Anna Sanderson writes about the world as she sees it (with the odd twist and turn). You can find her work online and in various zines and anthologies including 101 Words, Fifty Word Stories and Lights Go Out. Follow her story on social media at @annasanderson86.

MYNA WALLIN

Myna Wallin is a Toronto born poet and prose writer. The most recent of her three published books is Anatomy of An Injury (Inanna Publications, 2018). Wallin's poetry has appeared in Vallum, Quarantine Review, NōD Magazine, Sledgehammer, Miramichi Reader, Anti-Heroin Chic, and Antigonish Review among many publications both in Canada and the U.S. Wallin has a master's degree in English from the University of Toronto. Her poetry won two honorable mentions: for CV2 2-Day Best Poem Prize and the Winston Collins/Descant Prize for Best Canadian Poem. Wallin's poem, "Resurrections," was chosen for the 2018 League of Canadian Poets' Poem-in-Your-Pocket-Day. Myna had two poems long-listed in the 2022 Nick Blatchford Occasional Verse Contest.

ALSO FROM THE RED PENGUIN COLLECTION

POETRY

'Tis The Seasons – Poems to Lift Your Holiday Spirits
the flower shop on the corner – A Spring Poetry Anthology
the ocean waves – A Summer Poetry Anthology
the leaves fall – An Autumnal Poetry Anthology
Proud to Be – A Pride Poetry Collection
Words for the Earth – A Poetry Project

FICTION

What Lies Beyond – Sci-Fi Stories of the Future
I Can't Find My Flashlight – Contemporary Campfire Stories
A Heart Full of Love – A Collection of Romantic Short Stories
Behind Closed Doors – A Mystery Anthology
Once Upon A Time… – A Fairy Tale Anthology
Ernest Lived …and other Historical Fiction Short Stories
Until Dawn – A Supernatural Anthology
Treat-or-Trick – Halloween Horror Stories
Pets On the Prowl – An Animal Mystery Anthology
My Robot & Me – A Not-So Fiction Anthology

THE STAND OUT SERIES

Stand Out – The Best of The Red Penguin Collection, Vol. 1
Stand Out – The Best of The Red Penguin Collection, Vol. 2

www.ingramcontent.com/pod-product-compliance
Lightning Source LLC
Chambersburg PA
CBHW060614080526
44585CB00013B/829